WATERSHED

POEMS BY TYLER DILLOW

Stubborn Mule Press
Devil's Elbow, Missouri

Copyright © Tyler Dillow, 2022

First Edition: 1 3 5 7 9 10 8 6 4 2

ISBN: 978-1-958182-17-8

LCCN: 2022943469

Author photo: Hana Issa

Cover image: Joh Lee Grafton

Acknowledgments:

Some of the poems herein previously appeared in the following journals:

"Oat Milk & Other Alternate Endings" first appeared in *Olney Magazine.*

"Late June on the North Side of Town" first appeared in *Hobart.*

Special thanks to Tim Tarkelly and Luchador Press.

TABLE OF CONTENTS

Foreward

Promotional trends aside, there's no rule from the artist's side that says a book of poems must be a singular project rather than a mere collection of individual poems. I sometimes get nostalgic for an earlier time, one I was never part of, when I see old book titles like Poems 1926. A poet's poems written in any given span of years, however, tend to share certain themes and concerns, if for no other reason than just because they were written by the same person in the same period, the same heart and mind. The poet's task then in framing a collection is to identify the recurring concerns and make conscious and deliberate the preoccupations that may have merely been accidental and subconscious.

In his first volume, Tyler Dillow adroitly gathers his sundry poems together as a Watershed. A watershed is a perfectly conceived title to illuminate this particular collection, but we might also note that it is a perfect analogy for the unity that underlies any poetry collection. A watershed, in its American usage, is all the land whose snow and rainfall drains into the same body of water, and it includes both the networks of surface streams and the groundwater and subterranean aquifers that feed those streams. It thus represents the organic unity of a place, as defined not by political boundaries and human concepts, but by its intrinsic being and source. To apply the metaphor to the realm of poetry books: On the surface, we may identify a variety of subjects, modes, and themes (wildly divergent cities, towns, and principalities), but if there is a distinctive artistic intelligence flowing through the work, it will all share that source and move as one body of water.

In the case of Dillow's Watershed, one does not need to drill far beneath the surface to find that unity, particularly since, much as the watershed here works on several metaphorical levels at once, it is also literal. Yes, there is first the matter that these are often poems of origin and home, two of several available metaphors of "Watershed," but the childhood world referred to is not just figuratively a watery land of memory; it is also a land specifically characterized by an abundance of water. Water is invoked as an environmental milieu, as a source of food and economic sustenance, and almost as an elemental ancestor.

At the very least, the poet-speaker here comes from a farm in Kansas, but there is the suggestion of an almost mystical aquifer that defines the nature, wealth, history, and mythos of the land. Whatever the biographical world of the poet-speaker may be, it is rendered so as to be both concretely quotidian and mythically dream-like. This emerges most directly in the final poem of the collection, "Conservation," where "the knowing and not knowing [come] together to form a body of water on a piece of land—a watershed, a birth, a killing." And the speaker yields to and becomes this place, dreamily stepping "further into the water":

I am full as the water surrounds me. Swimming deeper, the rays of the sun wash over the fish and plants—I feel like the fish and plants. When they touch me, bubbles rise up around me.

It's all bubbles.
It's all plants and fish.

But if the biographical origins of water are not made explicit until the final poem, the centrality of water is apparent throughout the collection. Some element of water is present in nearly every poem. There are baths, pools, lakes, rivers and streams (and fish), basins and rain gullies, bubbles and buckets, saltwater, saliva, groves of fog, drops of blood, even condensation dripping from a tile ceiling. When water is not literally present in the scene, it nevertheless lurks in frequent verbs of liquidity (skim, spill, pour) and in the delectably moist foods that are either centerpieces or side events in poem after poem: juiced oranges, cracked eggs, eel sauce, cold jars of jam and tea, mashed apples, honeydew, Lambshead soup broth, popping oil. Everything seems to partake of the world of water, even ultimately the speaker subject and his beloved. "I spill into you / Take your shape" says the speaker of "The Shape of Me into You." And this universality of a shared element is even more present in "An Attempt to Move On," in which a "you" and "I" sit across a table and look into each other's eyes, as condensation falls from the ceiling, only to find in that room "more than two people sitting / ... / turns out we are everyone."

Water is traditionally associated with both emotion and sensuality, and its prevalence in the collection reflects the primacy of both forms of abundance here. The book is replete with invitations to small moments of pleasure, love, intimate community, and sensuous wonder. Some of these invitations are given in the form of recipes, recipes not only for a certain dish, but for an experience of how to best prepare or enjoy the dish with others, how to create and savor the moment. Other poems savor the sensual intimacy of sex and love itself. "Honey Blouse," a gorgeous poem, for example, begins "you call the act of love— / breaking horses / and when I don't agree it breaks you" and goes on to blend the sensuous world of food and the "undressing" of selfhood (and language) in sexual intimacy, concluding with the refrain of "honey blouse / honey home / honey honey." In "Body," light, water, and the body of a beloved all merge together, "overflowing / a spilling basin of god's fluids" at the end of Summer.

Likewise, Dillow insists on a ubiquitous presence of emotion, a vast water table beneath even the simplest moment, such that moving through the poems feels like moving through emotional bodies of water. But if, as Wallace Stevens suggested, cloying sentimentality arises not from being too emotional but from a failure of authenticity in emotion, then these poems are not really sentimental at all. Their authenticity derives perhaps from the unassuming manner in which the speaker inhabits emotional experience, almost as if it was one more form of sensuously undressing the self. One of the collection's most powerful poems is a water-saturated father-son poem of origin, "Leaving," in which the son takes on his father's shape as he elsewhere takes a lover's shape. The speaker, who also swims with and takes on the shape of the fish that will be served for dinner, concludes the poem:

. . . I know to come home
to the gutting. The gutting
table was my father's table
and he never said
my name, only water.

"My name, only water": in that final line we find not only one more figure for the poet-speaker's identification with water, but also a statement of poetics, the last dimension evoked in the title Watershed. Water is clear, transparent, plain, as is the voice that dominates this collection. For all its variety—ranging from the surreal "Falling Back in Love with You" to the halting (and haunting) syncopation of the companion pieces "I Am My [Mother's / Father's] Child"—Watershed offers a consistent aesthetic style that savors the moment (of thing; of emotion) plainly and nakedly, relishing the plainness, even the inadequacy, of the words that seek to hold it—even as the world's immanence keeps spilling out of language entirely.

-Sam Taylor
Wichita, Kansas
April 17, 2022

For Hana. For my family. For my friends.

A wild horse, a new tool, an eaten melon / Full of rainwater and tadpoles.

— Frank Stanford

Late June on the North Side of Town

We are in a paleteria eating lime & chamoy ice cream—
or is it sorbet? On our walk over we talked
about ginkgo leaves & how they offer the perfect
amount of shade for a porch & how we hate limestone

buildings, even if they could be nice—
which they aren't— why would you pick limestone?
It's hot out & we are in the shade.
You complain about forgetting socks
or how you aren't wearing the right shoes for walking.

You spoon-feed me the little chunks of lime
left in the ice cream & tell me, if you know what you're doing,
you drizzle chamoy over every bite. It's better.

It is better & we know, the bright green
& deep red spoonfuls mean more
than whatever building you end up in.

Boys of Summer

leftover on the pavement pieces of skin & little red
metal scraps, we tried to put together, that we

>   tried to glue, that we tried & you were still alive &
>   you were still the son of the sheriff—you still are

but it's not the same. the inversion of sunlight
against the concrete measures what needs to be done,

>   measures what happens, when you measure your
>   knees bent against the road & your legs wrapped

around one another, one another—a certain bicycle,
a certain stampede of rubbing together, a tire swing in

>   the backyard at your friend's house. his swing
>   became your swing & he held you together with

rope, which when broken down are tightened strings.
he didn't keep you at arms-length. he took you in

>   & you would float & he would take you.

Body

i let the sun fall down
over my body

a terra cotta basin
of light next to a pool

you dip your toes
you soak your feet

when i look at you
it's a terra cotta basin

filled and spilling

i trip and fall
over your body

you let me
and you are warm

so warm—overflowing

a spilling basin of god's fluids

a la fin de l'ete

Welcome Oranges

you look at me and the trees
next to us, next to me—

full, green, swaying limbs.

and i look at you when you say,
'this was my home.'

(the color of earth inside you)

and years later it still is.

the sun on your feet
shade from the trees.

we see the oranges in the light
we smell the citrus in the air.

the ground soft from rain
the day before—we step

we stand on the tips of our toes
to pull and pick the oranges.

you say,

(the world in your eyes)

here take this.

and i eat.
and i think,

this is your home.
pulling another orange
from the grove.

A Recipe on Making Eggs for Two

What is needed:

> -two people (happy together)
> -one pan, cast iron or nonstick
> -one spatula
> -two forks
> -one plate
> -three large eggs (preferably farm fresh)
> -salt

-black pepper

-hot sauce (optional or to taste)

> -one-third cup of butter

Now have one person heat the pan on the stovetop, while the other picks the music. Pick something light, airy, fun. Something you can both dance to. No pressure but this is an important step. If the right song isn't picked you could throw off the whole meal. Don't over think it. Pick what you know—it is not the time to test out new moves.

Person One: I haven't heard this song in forever.

If you're in charge of the pan, it is time to add the butter. Allow it enough time to melt. There is no need to watch it closely you will know when it is ready. Look into your partner's eyes, and you will probably notice they have their arms extended out to meet yours, let them take you. Dance to the music and the sound of butter melting.

Person Two: The butter melted.

But don't sound overly concerned. Be gentle and let them go cook and queue the next song. Any song by Al Green will do.

After the butter melts, crack the eggs, one-by-one, into the pan. Let them sizzle. Let them pop. Each one will take its own shape similar to the next but not exactly the same. This is okay. This is how it is supposed to go. Turn the heat down just a little and allow yourself to slip back into the moment. Sing to each other. Softly touch their shoulder. Walk up behind them and hug them. bring them close to you so they will know:

This is for you. It is all for you.

Someone say (it doesn't matter who): Wow, it smells so good in here.

Or something along those lines because, yes, by now your home will smell like warm butter and good music.

The eggs should almost be ready so bring out a plate. Just one. It is more fun to eat together. To share the meal and the moment in one continuous motion. This is something you both will appreciate. Something that neither of you can name—it is something you know. Use your spatula and remove each egg from the pan.

Person One: I can't wait any longer.

But you do wait. You wait to see the look on their face. A look brought on by the bright yellow yolks in the center of a soft outside. They know it is not the eggs that brings this look but the act of cooking and being together.

Person Two: grab the salt and pepper and hot sauce. Offer to salt, pepper, hot sauce the eggs, even though you and I both know their answer. Asking is the important part. Always ask. Always offer. Remember back, you are in this together.

Did you freshly squeeze orange juice? (Refer back to my other recipes for instructions.) If not, that is okay, say it's all sugar anyways, if they ask. Even though you and I both know it would have been good.

Person One: grab two forks and sit the plate on the table. Both of you sit down, next to each other, smile, and eat.

You make a mental note to make orange juice the next time.

What Happens When You Look at the Sky

i love the space in my brain
i dont even know

a weeping willow embanked
on a river

Pink From Earth

marble—pink and wet from rain

wet from wind.

pink from minerals

layered in the earth.

pink from embarrassment

pink blood in your mouth from grinding teeth

light red—pink from saliva

pink from pink

wet and warm

Falling Back in Love with You

She said, Watch this,
and I did. I watched
a masked woman place
a fawn into the mouth
of a carp and pulled it back
out again. She did this
over and over until the fawn
was you. My mouth
opening and closing.

Her hands pulled you
from my stomach
and I couldn't help,
but open my mouth
again.

Kansas

i miss people who don't miss me
and i miss people who do

cut me off

a kite flying high and let loose

A Good Year

The soybeans grew which made it a good year.

Walking along the hedgerow, I kick the fallen apples.

My great-grandmother told me, To plant these
    hedgerows was a lot of work.

She said, More work than you know.

They would take the apples, mash them in buckets,
and pour them into the smooth, deep trench they dug
by hand. The rows are miles long. The rows grid the
land. They make it square.

I kick the apples. I sing songs about hedgerows.

Hedgerows keep the dust away, but I sing to bring it in.

A bobwhite quail whistles and I whistle back. It's easy
to know it's a quail. It whistles its name—bobwhite.
And that's how I know, it whistles its name.

My father taught me this like fathers do when they
teach their kid something no one could know. Other
people do know, but I know what my father knows and
father knows this.

I sing a song about the quail and the rain begins to fall.

The danger with quail is where they lay their eggs.
In gullies and ditches, under brush and reeds.
So when it rains it can wash them away. And the
turkeys can stomp their eggs.

When it rains a lot can be washed away. That's the
problem with rain, but it makes for a good year
because the soybeans grow.

The prairie sways and I sing old songs.

I sing them loud and sway like the prairie sways.

Songs, people only sing in Kansas.

Songs that bring the dust in. I sing songs I was taught.
But when it rains I can't kick up dust.

My mother told me, It's best to sing these songs alone.

And I think it's best because only the wind can hear
you and the wind can carry. This is what she said, so
I let it carry me.

I can see the soybeans growing out in the field and
I can hear my father saying, It's going to be a good
year.

Eucharist

he held
a small
amount
of him

in his mouth

separating
pulp from
pulp from
mango to
nectarine

syrupy to
stagnant
sweet

Cultivation

i think of models
in scrunched up positions
naked against stones
boulders trees

knees and elbows
covered in dirt

dirt between their toes
under their nails

Caravaggio did this
and it was holy

naked pressed earth
mighty unholy
naked pressed earth

bare bare
marbolo smoke

champagne vinegar
to make an orchard
nude

and we're in this together
convoluted and complex

these bodies cold and wet

layer after layer of sheer

cut by scissors

thrown by hand
to make these bodies

more naked
than they already are

It's 3:00 A.M. and You're Outside

is it a cherry or an orange

floating above?

satellites skim
the atmosphere

you taste
sugar
in your tea

sugar in the air—

soft
sweet
cotton
candy

the air is thick
around you
a grove of fog

the air
the stars
the tea

it all tastes like—

saltwater
sugar
taffy

stretching over you

If I Saw You

persimmon robes
in the moonlight
are what you wear
when you want
to be left alone
to wear the moonlight

you want them to think
you look like neil young

i think you look like a feather
lifeless weightless
held together by your own self-image

and when you wear it
i leave you alone
a heavy persimmon
overripe useless

i couldn't help but see this—

and i see you
kissing
in my mirror

thinking about
what it would
look like if i saw you

What I Look Like in Pictures

my teeth whiter from not smoking
my teeth whiter from the toothpaste

i'd floss   gums bleeding
i'd floss   til i was pretty

               & i was pretty

i took up running
i took up chewing nicotine gum

it is all disgusting

& the more i run the more i hate my face

& the more uncomfortable i become with my body

in pictures i'd look better headless

or with no body at all

Gratification

you take my rib and run it through the dishwasher
          then the washing machine. you don't forget to
bleach it.

you don't forget—you want every body
          to know how pure things can be. you see my
bones

— white as the sun—

you cut open your stomach, bleed on the floor—
          it is your stomach, your knife, my rib.

you think my rib is yours to keep and store. you take it
          and shove it between two bones—

you believe any two will work. you take me and store me—
          any two won't work.

Allergy

I read when you eat
too much you feel it
in your feet. It starts
in your mouth—sore teeth
moving down sore feet.
arrogance made me
terrible. the words weren't
right—salamander, trout
bones, prayers for our family.
Your father's stories
sung together—a lack
of Vitamin B hung together
makes a person allergic
to bread. When trout
die, bacteria live
in their bloodstream—
when my friend died, they blamed
him. We couldn't teach
him how to live or
how to sing or how to love
misunderstandings. With three
shots to the chest,
Stanford taught us
about the moon and Lorca
taught me about sad guitars
and horses. When you read,
it changes once you look
away. It is not the same
all kept together, tiny

strings all tied
together. I held on
to certain advantages
like after I read this poem—
I didn't want to call it that.
We needed this—it was all
almost real.

When I Think About You,
I Think About Dinner

squash blossoms
and warm zucchini
slowly appear to be
worth eating. i crave
warm rice more than
i do red meat. your
father assures me this
isn't normal. i make
eel sauce. it doesn't
contain eel. heat soy
sauce in a pan and add
sugar. let the sugar
dissolve, then pour it
over rice. when i
say squash, I mean
my body. craving
the deep nasal spice
of wasabi and your
hand over my mouth

Cocoon

i eat the hand off the palm of your neck
bringing you in closer—and closer
and closer. In the room smothered
by the smooth scent of moonlight—
i find you and your eye follows me
across the bridge, so i crossover.

you comb my hair, fingers brush
my forehead. you're polished—silk
cream. let me kiss your neck
and let your hands grip my thighs.
this is how it should be, this is

how it is. my hand covers your mouth
and muffled noise slips through
my fingers—warm saliva.
my palm, your mouth,
on hands and knees feeling for more.
close your eyes—i close mine—feel

the slow pull of gravity on your body.
it's baffling how bodies meet,
how they come together to form
the warm cocoon of a skyline.

Cicadas

a cicada's shrill cry pours through my window.
a cicada screams into heaven.
i cover my ears. legs move across my ears—
i hear crickets. crickets rub their legs.
children are made by rubbing legs
and shouting to heaven. listen close—
with my eyes i see, with my hands i see—no.
i see my eyes whored out—my eyes heart
cicadas and the body around me.
inside, the clothes hangers on my bedroom floor
are next to my socks and my socks are next to my bed
in my bedroom and next to the opal ghost sur-
rounding me. i look out the window—dark.

Theology of Sugar

I gave you two red spoonfuls of jam
And you handed me a pot of tea.

And now, you tell me— it's April,
So if April, what if April. I say, the younger months must
    be much sweeter.

In this moment, we are made of jelly
And with the prick of an ice pick—

We all spill out.

And if hands sweep us up to be made
Into sugar—we'd taste like watermelon.

Spooning the sugar into tea, I say—

My Father, when you were younger the tea was sweeter.
My Father, it's spring and all things are meant to be
    seduced.
My Father, what intimacy it brings.

please stay close.

Dear God,

spoon me back together.

Offering

And this is me fingering the ribs of God,
my hands bronze-tipped spears
reflect warm blood orange, a simmering
heart warmed sun, heated blood
in a bowl.

I stir the broth as it boils
pulling a lamb's head from it.
We peel meat off the boiled head.
We see bone. I take a knife
and pry in between the eyes
and the bone cracks,

Morrissey croons in the kitchen.
He, a soldier, dies
in the kitchen. His hands left
in the sink. I wash them.

We bury Morrissey in the backyard,
he sings through our Walkman.
We take turns passing the headphones.
On repeat. Repeat the whole night. His songs.
His hands left in the sink, clean.

The lamb's head on the counter
sings along. White, pearly white,
blinding white. I make its teeth
into a necklace and sharpen its
jawbone into a knife. He's dead,

but here I am. Singing and smooth
the opal bones of God
thumbing against my fingers.

Cleaning Up Together

You folded your hands and I wore a dress
and swept dust out from under the table.

You folded your hands like you folded me.
Each hand touched each shoulder.
Each ankle touched each ankle,
but I was sweeping.

Picking up dust, wiping the counter,
folding you in my eyes like you were folding me.

You folded me on the table.

You touched my neck.

I was a dress you liked to fold.

You Look So Good in Blue

For Frank Stanford

He shook the blood off his jacket.
Standing on the dried river bank,
the heart of a fawn beat
in his left hand. Beat,
beat more.

He dusted salt over it.
He'd left home. He never
thought about his father.
The fawn moved in the dirt.

Silver snakes crawled in its belly.
His teeth like pearly gates gashed
open the heart. He chewed and
spit and chewed arteries,
cartilage, and lean
muscle as caviar.

He thought about the daughters
of the river and bellowed
their names, eroded soil.
Gum roots like tongues of mothers,

He lied to all the fathers.

He shucked away the rind of cold melon,
God's fingernails, the moon filled
an empty bowl placed in the far corner.

His eyelash fell and milk
thistle erupted.

He drew a dotted-line.
His toes rooted in the shore.

Leaving

Small drops of blood
led me to the gutting
table. My father wasn't home
everyday. In the summer,
we ate well. I mean, if you didn't
mind bread and butter, rice
and fish. My whole life
I watched him,
mimicked him. I'd put on
his belt, his hat,
march around the house,
then outside. Outside, where he
walked, I walked, soon he followed.
I'd wipe the table. Wash it clean.
Wait for him to finish
scrub again.
Now I swim around the lake.
I watch the fish below me.
And swim like them. We swim,
together. Through the trees,
I still feel it. Across the lake,
I feel it. I know to come home
to the gutting. The gutting
table was my father's table
and he never said
my name, only water.

An Attempt to Move On

i'm afraid of the living
more than i am the dead
more than i am of dying

you sit at the table
across from me

we look into each other's eyes
we look into each other
when we do we see

more than two people sitting

condensation builds on the tile ceiling
until it drops onto the floor

turns out we are everyone

Tomato Living

if i wanted to live
i'd be a sun-dried tomato

picked by hand
picked by a grandmother
left to dry in the sun

when i'm covered
in olive oil
red draped in orange

alive in a glass jar
preserved
to be eaten

place me in water
boil me home

it bubbles
and i'm sealed
into living

placed on a shelf
to collect
to be eaten

to be shared on a plate
in the shade of a summer day

the wind blows
and i'm swallowed
gone

Wasting Time

everyday i pushed
a red wheel-barrow
and broke green glass
on fresh concrete.

i looked at it—
sparkling and wet
through a window
of a dog food plant
down the road.

i let rain fill buckets
i let rain collect
on framed pictures
of friend and family.

i spent the summer
reading William Carlos Williams
only to learn—

i can't write.

Learning a Lesson

you and i look over our daughter, our son, our person
& say be safe. to say, be safe, is an understatement.
forgiving parents is a different kind of empathy—
so we prepare lentil soup or chicken & spinach,
they eat it with a spoon, then leave the house to go
out with friends & we stay home praying we taught
them right & when they get home, we cube fresh melon,
place it in a bowl, & share it as a family. when you think
of your parents, you don't think of their smile or the list
of chores they leave for you to finish, while they work.
you recall the sharp-scent of garlic in your home
as soup boils on the stovetop or the pale green of honeydew
& how they teach you to bite into a raw pepper,
after your first mouthful of chicken. & later, much later,
much much later— in your own kitchen as you lay thin slices
of eggplant into hot oil, by hand, you hear their voices—
be safe, & the oil pops as it fries.

In the Kitchen

i opened a cold mason jar of jam spread it thick
across burnt toast—warm & crisp,
the raspberry jam cool against my tongue.
& on the roof of my mouth, i tasted the work
of my mother's hands—jam sweet, so sweet
sucrose sweet. in the pot boiled refined sugar &
raspberries & when you stir them with a wooden
spoon they become one. if you were here, in the kitchen
my mother would say—don't sift the seeds out,
they are important for you to taste.

Holding On

my father grabbed my shoulders and shook me
like a father does when he is mad with love
and i looked at him. Looked him in the eye
as the vibration ran through my body
and i saw pink and red well up in his eyes
and the stress in his knuckles. these are my hands,
these are the same hands—the same hands that taught
me to tie fishing lure to line and the same arms that
taught me to cast and when i'd catch a fish, we'd toss it
back—occasionally, we'd keep it.

I Am My Mother's Child

My mother told me   stay close   stand
         next   to me I will   I will always
love you love the way you stand   next
to   me as long as   as   long as you
stay store   yourself at the center
             of God I would   tell her
the only time   the only time I talk
     to God   is with my   hands and trust
trust me   Mother   it's not intentional
         because   I may be aligned
but   I see
                 God I see   I see   God how
Caravaggio saw   saints   cow-eyed and   moony
             With dirt between   dirt between
their
toes and intoxicated   with moon-pie faces unable
         to speak   to   speak   to   speak
Mother   when mothers say stay close   they mean
         leave   but don't   leave don't   leave my
             don't leave God out   of your
life
out of   your living   out   of your
speaking so
I tell   her   I won't   I won't talk   to
God
 or build
     an altar but I will   I   will live   within a
tabernacle of   animals I don't tell her
 I won't believe   but I   will and when I speak to
         her   I use   my hands and   when I

speak to her   I spell her   name which in
my
       doughy eyes   my doughy
face
spells   God

I Am My Father's Child

Father   father   violence stores   itself inside
      of me   stores itself   inside
bone
                    because
how   does my   skeletal structure
hold   what was passed   on to   me my Father-
    father told me pass   it on   into the
ether
            let the arms   on both sides
            of your body   carry over father Father
my anger is   a son
your arms   swing too   low in the
strokes
of Rivera and blot out   your   father Father

in the   vigorous strokes of a   communist
            because
all communists store   a wealth of aggression
            in the cavity   of their
                                            chest
between
            both arms   Father-   father
tell me
            what father   told you
to tell   me

                                    you
know what to say

A list of things that couldn't possibly be mine,
but are

A lamp with no lampshade
An exposed wire
The dented corner of a coffee table

Being naked in the bathtub
Naked on the stairs and in the bed
A patchwork quilt on the floor

Hair clogging a drain
Leftover coffee grounds on a counter
Cigarette butts in a glass high heel

Scuffed hardwood floors
An overripe banana
An open window's torn curtains

Incense strong enough to kill a priest
A rusty pocketknife
Puddles of water in a parking lot

Emotional unavailability
An unused book of stamps
Burnt out lightbulbs

A stack of wine bottles meant for recycling
Rotting lemons
Unanswered text messages

Clean white towels
Your shirt
An unmade bed

The color blue
The crescent shaped phase of the moon
Brown fast food napkins

The way you laugh at me
A broken clock
An elementary school's gymnasium

A vhs copy of Jurassic Park
A picture of you in love
An uncooked almond croissant

Going Blank Feeling Blank

each person tells you how special you are
they say this and do this
until you don't feel special anymore

dogtooth
tepid water on a night stand
ice cold strawberries on your lips

when you think about _____

you put cherry-chapstick on
before you let go
a saddlebag hung on a hook
a sawhorse
breaking the seal on cheap nail polish

your stomach is upset
this is what makes you
special

bruised knees bruised elbows bruised peaches
everybody on their knees
each person a cold island drink

the people from dinner are around you now
they tell you how special you are
and what kind of person you could be

you go _____

and when you think about feeling sad
you don't feel anymore

a finished slice of watermelon
a piano string
rainier cherries in a bowl

you letting go until you aren't _____

anymore

Before There was Much More

we microdose and eat croissants

the water in the pool is clean

don't stop me from keeping you, i say

it's bitter cold for the spring

this was before when we could eat gluten

you see the darkwood cabinets of your childhood

we're not brought into this

home

how else does one move on

you perhaps—now

move through high thread

count sheets

or clumsy dives

i tell you i want to swim

you begin to talk and it is not

the words i don't understand

but your mouth and how it moves

you bring me my black sweater

i say this all to you and you say

we're going out

could it be the corinthians over the doors of the

house

too ornate for someone with good taste

then again it all feels

good

thought up by someone who is not me

we still microdose

                now it's just considered dropping

you vomit in the pool

                  we start our day

we swim

Off the Coast

worn down mercedes take me home
i drink coffee tea and eat desserts

covered in rose water syrup it sticks
to my chin they pour fresh

asphalt onto the road outside the car
intoxicate me the sweet scent of citrus

under my nails from eating oranges
bommali welcome me palm frond

i am
sundown
windows down
home

Honey Blouse

you call the act of love—

        breaking horses

and when i don't agree it breaks you

i grab the collar of your shirt and unbutton the button

the top button unbuttoned and it all comes undone

when i say honey blouse

        i mean

sharing slices of peach from a bowl
the arch of my nose pressed into you
licking icing off a chocolate cake

        is undressing

        honey honey

we find a way to break horses

and stomp mad in the house

burning down around us

honey blouse

honey home

honey honey

Oat Milk & Other Alternate Endings

you tousle your hair, messy hair, hair fringed & torn
            to breaking. when i say you

i mean me. myself, in a bathtub of lukewarm water,
            all the bubbles gone, stagnant, trying to
sleep.

            sugar, caffeine, the hot water you rushed to
heat before
you got here. maybe, you should have added dairy

            or some sort of milk alternative, before now.
before you placed your foot

in the water followed by your legs,
            your whole body. not your head.

            think the straight cut of scissors across your
forehead,
your hair collapsing onto your naked lap, think about
you

and not me. think about
            ladybugs on an april morning or boys

in late june, who wear golden yellow
            swim trunks. perhaps consider spooning

            as an alternative to fucking
or the logical next step.

or how in yourself there is more
            than this iced coffee with oatmilk

            you accidentally spilled in the bath,
so you could fuck with your hair.

is the light in this room too bright? was this even
            a good idea? would the boys

or the ladybugs even recognize you?

The Shape of Me into You

there's a heart-shaped pillow
bedazzled and breathtaking
in the shape of your arms

you wear red lipstick
you wear a night dress
that wears you

like a red coat in a cold room
we come together
your arms fold over my sides

i spill into you
take your shape
your hair falling

over my shoulders
look at how close we are
look at how we take

the same shape

look

at how wonderful it is to be alive
and waste all the time you want
kissing

Paella or How to Host a Dinner Party

sweat onions and red peppers in a pan.
add fish stock and rice—
spanish rice —then add more fish stock.

cover the pan and talk. talk about dessert,
 ask if anybody wants a drink—does anybody want a
    drink?
muddle strawberries and honey to mix with champagne
    and gin.

take in the moment—before you add clams
and mussels and langoustine—to appreciate
how your friend parts their hair. it's parted to the left.

now as you think about your friends, ask them—
do you ever think of me?
then place the clams, mussels, and langoustine in the rice.

let it simmer

in the stock— your friends won't know what to say,
 so don't forget to top the dish with saffron.

your friends will be a little drunk—
they won't notice if you forget. serve the dish
and ask again—do you ever think of me?

Citrus

it's cold, all the lemons are dead, i imagine your hand,
your arm, your body reaching for them & me.

this is the making of grief—my legs, my thighs, my torso
climbing the step ladder. you raking the fallen citrus.

all the lemons are dead. i take my shirt off. it couldn't be
more perfect, more self-conscious—this is the making

of desire. your cheek brushes against the hair
on my stomach. i pull at the branches of the tree

& fall from the step ladder. leaves fall, we are on
the ground, & leaves fall. the lemons are dead,

instead we pick pomegranates. this is the making of reality,
the making of two people falling into each other. fuck me,

i'm sad. fuck me & my forgetfulness. i couldn't write out
the sadness of the lives around me. forgive me, forgive

mothers, forgive yourself. forgive us—we couldn't forget
how happy everyone around us was.

In the Garden of your Home

behind a row of olive trees sits a small plot of graves.

everything is green. trees form a canopy above us.
flowers and herbs and all things green grow here.

we talk about how sage is commonly grown around tombs,
we talk about what it must be like to hold onto something

so private in the garden of your home. the transference
of energy from one life to the next. it is all soft—the olive

trees, the sage, the act of burying who you love. all this
energy carrying over to where we are now. together,

we pick the sage to take home and make tea later.

Trace the Words

on a tuesday afternoon in the shade
the air smells of sage around us

i touch the burial stones
i trace the words
written in smooth black ink
carved into hard white marble
i think it is the words that matter here

i see you touch the stones
you tell me later

                    and only later

memories are easier to understand
when you're with them
you trace the words
and it's the people that matter

it's the people that matter
and how the words hold them together
underneath our hands
i say your name
the way they would have said your name

you tell me, it's time to go
we leave behind the shade
and sage in order to
carry each person we know

Calling Home by its Name

i hold the painted turtle in my hand.
the sun is out, it is a summer afternoon,
and i want to keep the little turtle.

in my house i find a box and fill it
with grass, stones, leaves, sticks.
the turtle needs to feel at home.

i put a small dish of water in the corner
with a few slices of cucumber.
i name the turtle a name only i could.

it is home.

my parents tell me, you can't keep it.
it will die here. this is not its home.
a box is no home for a turtle.

i understand but out there is no place
for a baby turtle. out there it can be
eaten by a bullhead or largemouth bass.

out there it has no name
and i think a named turtle can't die.
a named turtle can't be eaten.

it can always return, the way i do,
to the banks of the pond.
it can be here. it can be home.

i told them this and knew it was true.

in the morning, i take it to the bank of the pond
and let it go. i think a named turtle can't be eaten.
i think a named turtle can't die.

Conservation

Knee deep in water, tadpoles circle my ankles, and moss
floats by green and blue. My bare feet cool as tadpoles
move, back-n-forth, touching my toes. Standing here, it's
not easy to tell you, I want it all to go away.

I step forward—

the water comes to my thighs and it's cold and I feel cold.
Help me. Scoop the water up.
Help me. Hold my hands above my head. Open them for
me. Let the water fall through my hair and into my eyes.

Is falling apart an attempt to be healed—no. Not a
defensive no. Not the kind of no that means yes or kind
of, even though you, or me, would never say yes. People
like us are so quick to say no.

We are so quick to not believe.

Think back. You were told your family owned this
land. For a long time it meant nothing, then it meant
something. It meant you had something to hold onto.
Something to look forward to giving away. Something
that was never yours or your family's. This piece of land
like the tadpoles in the pond has always been here.
Scoop more water and drink it.

Taste what it means to lose without loss. Linger on how
giving and forgiveness, as an action, can be the same
thing. They can taste the same way. Clinging to my legs
are thick pieces of moss like you and me—blue and

green. Help me apply them as bandages. These wounds, un-healing. The wounds—I don't want, but they feel the same as water. They are what make water—water. I've been broken here before.

Two decades ago, my grandfather stood here. He asked the Kansas dirt to forgive him and it made him a farmer. Now, he's dirt. But he needed water to make a body and a body to cultivate the earth—this is community. He isn't here. When I was younger, I don't know what I said to him, but I know he held my hand and we walked. I know what you know. And what I do know is he stood here and asked the ground to take him—

he said, this is community.

The knowing and not knowing coming together to form a body of water on a piece of land—a watershed, a birth, a killing. I think about the water touching my knees because the water touched his knees the same. He was tall and had big hands perfect for working dirt.

You ask me—what did he think of the land? What did he think?

I'd like to tell you he only thought of God or that he only thought of preservation. I'd like that because it's hard to grasp. It's lost. It would mean the watershed was born innocent and the watershed only holds innocence. But I only know what he left and what he left is told to me by others.

I step further into the water—we step further.

I am full as the water surrounds me. Swimming deeper, the rays of the sun wash over the fish and plants—I feel like the fish and plants. When they touch me, bubbles rise up around me.

It's all bubbles.
It's all plants and fish.
It's all what I make it and what I want it to be.

It is all what they will it to be.

Tyler Dillow lives in Kansas. His work can be read in *Hobart, X-R-A-Y, Olney Magazine,* and elsewhere.